Regarding

Robinson R22

Helicopters

H H Brutlag

metloc
printers

British Library Cataloguing in Publication Data. A catalogue record for this book is available from the British Library.

ISBN 0-9540361-1-5.   ISBN(13 digit) 978-0-9540361-1-9.

Published by Rennsport Sidecars, 34 Coborn Street, London E3 2AB United Kingdom.

Acknowledgements:
First and foremost thanks to Frank Robinson for granting me an interview which proved to be candid, fascinating and fun. Kurt Robinson took time out of a busy day at Helitech to talk to me for which I am most grateful. Tim Tucker has generously allowed me to use information he presented during the Robinson Safety Course. Loretta Conley, Robinson PRO, confirmed facts and furnished the photos of 001 and 002. Randy Rowles kindly permitted me to use the photo on page 122.

Although every effort was made to confirm the contents of this book, apologies if any errors slipped through.
The information in this book is presented in good faith, but is not a substitute for professional helicopter training. The author and publisher disclaim any liability arising directly or indirectly from the use or misuse of this book.

On the front cover is serial number 1874, a 1991 R22 Beta, still young looking and going strong after three rebuilds.

Contents

Introduction

I designed the R22 purely as a personal helicopter.
Frank Robinson

The Robinson R22 helicopter can change your life.

It changed my life. I suppose you could say that it was learning to fly that changed my life, but really these become one and the same thing - the change becomes inseparable from the instrument of change.

How does the R22 do this? Why does it engender such deep feelings tied to personal identity?
It's a puzzle, yet...

What helicopter is so basic yet so beautiful, so delightful yet so demanding, so familiar yet so fresh, so sensitive yet so simple?

The Robinson R22 helicopter -
it's a personal helicopter in more ways than one.

Models

A new aeroplane does not just happen.
It is the result of thousands of hours of hard work.
Air Marshall Sir John Nelson Boothman
Empire Test Pilots' School Syllabus

The first prototype R22, serial number 001, was ready to fly in 1975. It was wheeled out of the ex-World War II tin hut hangar at Torrance Airport in August of that year. Frank Robinson prepared to take it through its first start-up and system checks. Two years earlier he had resigned his job at Hughes Helicopters and staked all his time and money on a dream of producing an inexpensive lightweight helicopter for everyman. It was now crunch time. Frank must have had his fingers crossed that it would work. Wrong. "I knew that it would work! I had a lot of experience by then."

The plan was to wait until the next day before attempting to lift into a hover for the first time. But, with everything working properly on the run-up, there seemed little point in waiting. So Frank cautiously "flew" 001 for the first time the same day.

Once the R22 was deemed ready for proper flight tests, a test pilot, Bob Golden, was engaged. He took 001 on its arduous journey towards certification. Unfortunately, it never got there.

During one of its flights the first ever R22 experienced lack of tail rotor efficiency. Bob had to autorotate and ditch in the Pacific Ocean near the Robinson base at Torrance. The R22, registered N67010, sank to the bottom.

Happily, both pilot and aircraft were safely recovered. The tail rotor was then examined and the fault ascertained. The component was strengthened, but not on 001. It was too badly damaged. A new R22 had to be built.

It was this R22, serial number 002, registration N32AD, that received certification by the FAA on 16 March 1979. It survives, safe and dry, in the care of the Smithsonian National Air & Space Museum at Dulles Airport in Washington D.C. When Frank Robinson presented it to the museum it had done nearly 6,000 hours of flight time including years of flight testing.

The next R22 built, 003, was the first one built to be sold. Finding customers for the R22 was not difficult. Even before 003 was built, there was already a backlog of orders for this new two-seater.

In October 1979 The Robinson Helicopter Company sold its first product: R22 serial number 003. The base price of $40,000 somehow turned into a delivery price of $48,000 for the first customer, Tim Tucker.

This was the **Standard** model R22 which was approved on 16 March, 1979. Fitted with a 150 horsepower Lycoming 0-320-A2B engine, de-rated to 124 hp, it had a gross weight of 1300 pounds even. This model ran from serial number 002 to 0199, not including 0175.

From serial number 0200 to 0255, 0257 to 0300, 0302 to 0349, and 0352 to 0356, and 0175, a 160 hp 0-320-B2C engine was fitted, also derated to 124 hp. These R22s were called the **HP** model and required 100LL aviation gasoline.

The **Alpha** model was available from October 1983 at a price of $77,850. The gross weight was increased to the now familiar 1370 pounds. These ran from serial number 0357 to 0500, including 0256, 0301, 0350 and 0351. And if you purchased one after January 1985 it might well have been fitted with the optional new auxiliary fuel tank increasing endurance by more than 60%.

Frank Robinson's dream became tangible with the construction of his first helicopter, above. It looks little different from today's product, apart from the shorter skids and shallow fanwheel. Below is serial number 002, the R22 prototype which eventually obtained FAA Certification in March of 1979. Today it resides at the National Air and Space Museum in Washington D.C.

When an auxiliary fuel tank is fitted it occupies the empty space opposite the main tank. Without the extra 10 gallons, an hour or so of endurance is sacrificed. However, there is improved access to the components visible above. The main rotor gearbox, oil level site window, Telatemp, jackshaft and push-pull tube assemblies are all visible and accessible.

A topped-up auxiliary fuel tank adds 65 pounds in extra weight. Add in the weight of the tank itself and fittings and there may well be a saving of 70 pounds or more without one. On a hot day at altitude, weight saving may be more important than endurance. In such a situation you may think that an Alpha model without the auxiliary tank, but fitted with the later more powerful Beta II 0-360 engine would be just the job. Unfortunately it cannot be done because the two models have their own individual aircraft Type Approval Certificates.

The HP model above resides at the Helicopter Museum courtesy of Heli Air Ltd. The early cyclic grip handle is moulded hard plastic. Mariners sometimes end up with floats removed, doing land duty.

With the introduction of the R22 **Beta** in August 1985 the instrument panel was enlarged from 5 to 7 holes. The price also enlarged to $85,850. The engine was still the 0-320-B2C derated to 124, but with a five minute take-off rating of 131 hp. Beta models ran from serial number 0501 to 2570.

Also introduced in 1985 was a Beta model fitted with floats. It carried the battery in the nose and received extra corrosion protection. Available to order from September 12th, **Mariner** models carry serial numbers with the suffix **M** in the eligible range 0501 to 2570 and 0364.

There was also a fully instrumented version of the R22 available in the Alpha, Beta and Beta II. The 10 hole instrument panel can seem quite large and intrusive when you are used to the usual basic 7. They are also slightly nose heavy which is noticeable when you pick up. These IMC models tend to fetch higher prices as they can be in demand for instrument training.

With a production run of more than ten years and 2000 aircraft, the Beta made Robinson the world's leading producer of light helicopters. That was at the end of 1988. An improved Beta, the **Beta II** was introduced in January 1996. It uses the Lycoming 0-360-J2A engine with 180 hp, de-rated as usual. Beta II serial numbers run from 2571 onwards.

A **Mariner II** version of the Beta II was also marketed from January, 1996. With the indicative **M** suffix they were available in the serial number range 2571 through 3414.

Since the discontinuation of the instrumented model and the Mariner, the choice of R22 is today greatly simplified: you can have any model you want as long as it's the Beta II. However, there is a choice of extras ranging from full 7 instruments plus GPS to leather seats and factory bubble windows. The Robinson web site has an interactive paint choice page which previews all the base and colour trim combinations available. They also offer metallic colours, but you really need to see them on the machine to appreciate the quality of finish.

Oftentimes people want to update their model to make it look like the current range of the product. However, after a certain number of years the older model becomes more unique and desirable if it is in its original form. This has happened with the Beta colour scheme with its repeated colour bands and **R22** logo in relief.

There were, of course, a number of milestones along the way. By April 1989 Robinson had produced 1000 R22s. At the end of the year it proved to be the most popular aircraft sold, outselling all other helicopters and airplanes. During 1999 R22s were so popular that production was heading towards the 3000 mark. Then in October, 1999, Sloane Helicopters in Northamptonshire took delivery of R22 serial number 3000. By early 2006, R22 serial number 4000 was on its way to Australia.

What made and still makes the R22 so sought-after? Reliability, amongst other things. And some of this is down to the choice of engine. Notwithstanding the relative complexity of the four stroke piston power-plant, much of the R22's reliability is down to the choice of this engine.

This is the 5 hole instrument cluster as fitted to serial number 0404, which is roughly mid way through the Alpha model range. Note the vertical arrangement of warning lights.

Placed side by side, below, the wider 7 hole housing has horizontal warning light arrangement across the top. The up-curve over the centre gives it a more balanced pleasing shape than the rather utilitarian 5 hole version. R22 changes over the years have been fairly subtle.

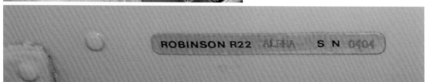

The ten hole instrument panel seems to obstruct your view forward until you get accustomed to it. The Instrument Flight Rules (IFR) model is in demand for instrument training, although the R22 is of course a Visual Flight Rules (VFR) only helicopter. On the left is a typical Beta II cluster with all 7 holes filled, VOR fitted, and a GPS console mounted on top.

Recent modifications to R22 instrumentation include a new warning light, fourth from left, indicating carbon monoxide presence.

New rounded tip caps on the end of the tail rotor help to quiet them. Frank Robinson applied his exceptional tail rotor knowledge when he first designed the R22. His design gave more thrust, so that it is hard to run out of left pedal in the R22.

Above: The vertical heat scoop held on with 6 screws indicates that this is a 0-320 engine. The 0-360 engine, below, fitted to the Beta II has a horizontal scoop held on with two clamps. The heat scoop deflects warm air from the exhaust pipe via the short orange coloured hose into the air cleaner. When the pilot pulls on carb heat, this pre-warmed air enters the carburettor instead of outside air in order to prevent carb icing. On the Beta II carb heat is correlated with the collective. Lowering collective adds carb heat and raising collective reduces it. The pilot may override this if desired.

Inside the Robinson hangar at Torrance, these new or newly rebuilt helicopters await collection. As the above photo suggests, Robinson currently sell more 44s than 22s.

Training schools often recycle their timed-out R22s rather than buy new. Accidents, of course, may necessitate a new replacement. The accident that wrecks the most R22s is the dynamic rollover. The pilot usually walks away, but the aircraft is mostly scrap.

Colour choice and conspicuousness: where do you want to be most visible, on the ground or in the air? Watching a black helicopter on final, it stands out well against a pale sky. Once it descends below the tree line it suddenly becomes invisible. The opposite is true of a white helicopter. Does the white helicopter in the above line-up stand out?

Whatever colour is chosen, an R22 will always be a rather small speck in a big sky, so it is best to keep a good lookout and not rely on others to spot you.

Engine

> He put this engine to our ears, which made an incessant noise like that of a water-mill; and we conjecture it is either some unknown animal, or the god that he worships; but we are more inclined to the latter opinion.
>
> Jonathan Swift,
> *Gulliver's Travels*

A worshipful attitude towards the engine is not altogether out of place. Yes, a helicopter will glide should the engine fail, and unlike an airplane it can land in a small area, but the aim is to keep the engine in tiptop order so that it has no reason to fail. For it is not just that an engine can fail, it can partly fail. And this can catch you off guard perhaps more than a complete failure. But more of that later. First, let's look at the engine itself.

The R22 was always going to be powered by a piston engine. That was Frank Robinson's original idea and it was based on years of experience as an engineer in the helicopter industry.

Makers of turbine-engine helicopters argue that turbines are simpler, have fewer moving parts and are more reliable. Large turbine engines as used by the airlines are indeed very reliable. But, small turbines fitted to helicopters were much less reliable.

They admittedly produce more horsepower, but in so doing run at high revolutions per minute. In addition, that much power going through the gearbox tends to produce more gearbox failures. So the well established Lycoming four cylinder piston engine was chosen. Its power output was de-rated so that Lycoming could agree to extend its total running time before overhaul.

Anyone who has owned a Volkswagen Beetle (the original one) will be familiar with the Lycoming range of flat four engines: horizontally opposed, 4 cylinder, four stroke engines cooled by air, not liquid. Avoiding liquid coolant saves weight (and no anti-freeze for the owner to worry about in winter). Both engines employ a carburettor fuel system, but whereas the VW uses battery-coil ignition, the Lycoming for safety and reliability reasons fits two independent magnetos with two spark plugs per cylinder head. Should one magneto fail the engine will continue to run. Hence the two magneto checks during start-up procedure.

The VW Beetle was legendary for its reliability. It had a relatively large capacity engine which ran at low rpm. The same principle is applied in the Lycoming. The Lycoming 320 power-plant produces 150 horsepower at 2700 rpm on the early Standard R22s. This increased to 160 hp on the subsequent R22s, until the Beta II. It is fitted with the 0-360 model motor of 180 hp, but de-rated to 145.

All of the engines fitted were de-rated. But, why deliberately give up horsepower that is there for the taking? Because what you lose in power, you gain in reliability and durability. And there is less strain on the drive train. So the 320 engine is de-rated to 124 hp, and the 0-360 to 145 hp. Robinson set up the manifold pressure gauge so that only 131 hp out of the 180 is used. This ensures gentle use and longevity for this relatively large engine.

The progressive selection of engines with greater horsepower has enabled the R22 to better cope with high density altitude. The 150 hp engine is full throttle at 3,700 feet, the 160 hp is full throttle at 5,800 feet, whereas the Beta II engine of 180 hp uses full throttle at 8,500 feet, all at 20° C. In hot climates such as in Florida and Southern California where temperatures of 30 degrees are routine, the extra capacity can take some of the stress out of steep approaches and maximum performance take-offs.

Lycoming nomenclature indicates the actual engine cubic capacity in inches. Hence the 0-320 engine is 320 cubic inches and the 0-360 is 360 cubic inches or 5900 cubic centimetres. This is a large capacity engine from which to take only 131 horsepower. Compare, for example, the Lycoming 0-360 engine of 5900cc to another similar engine of half the capacity.

Maker	Model	Capacity	Horse-power	Fuel octane	Oil held	Vne
Lycom-ing	0-360-J2A	5900cc	145 @ 2700	100	6 US quarts	102knots 118mph
Porsche	911 SC	2994cc	195 @ 5900	98	13.7US quarts	127knots 146mph

Compared with other engine configurations these two air-cooled horizontal engines, each famous in their own way, have a great deal in common. Yet, note the differences. The Lycoming engine despite having twice the capacity of the Porsche develops 50 horsepower less. It is not hard to see why.

Lycoming are aiming for fail-safe reliability. So the pistons revolve at less than half the speed of the Porsche. Of course the Porsche does have two more pistons and fuel injection. It is aiming for high performance, without trading off too much of their famous reliability; whereas for the engine powering the R22, reliability is paramount.

Porsche engines should last for 100,000 miles or more before requiring an inspection or a rebuild. If you take 50 mph as an overall average speed during that time, and divide 100,000 miles by 50 miles per hour you end up with 2000 hours running time. Add in 10% standing still time and the result is 2200 hours, the precise rebuild requirement figure for the Lycoming engine.

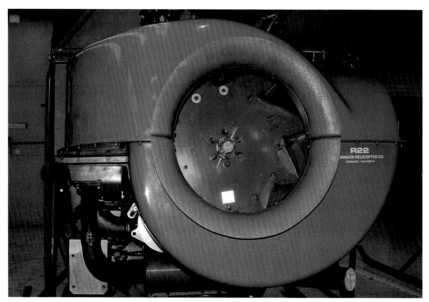

The R22 has plenty of space to accommodate a large fan and ducting. The air cooling for the Porsche must be squeezed into an engine bay of very limited size. (The black plastic container above the fan is not part of cooling, it is the air cleaner). Hence the Porsche relies on twice the volume of oil to help keep things cool.

The difference is that the Lycoming engine in the R22 *must* be removed, inspected, and rebuilt as necessary. Whereas there is no statutory requirement to remove and inspect the Porsche engine at 2200 hours. Whether it is running like clockwork, or alarmingly, it can carry on as before.

Notwithstanding that the Porsche produces more power per cubic centimetre, there is more to performance than raw power. The 911 SC is quite a heavy lump to shift. Fully laden at 1500 kg it has a power to weight ratio of 7.69 kg / hp. The R22 with a maximum weight of just 621 kg has only 4.28 kg / hp. So the R22 makes good use of the available power.

The comparison with a Porsche engine is not as eccentric as it might appear. Porsche actually produced aero engines which were apparently fitted to some Mooney and Cessna fixed wing aircraft. But the potential market for aero engines is slight compared to cars and of course being Porsche they were never going to be cheap. So despite being advanced for their time, they were discontinued.

Safety

Just because an accident does not happen, that does not automatically mean that a system is safe. Likewise, the occurrence of an accident does not prove that a system is unsafe.

> Paul A. Craig,
> *The Killing Zone*

The primary causes of accidents in the R22 have shifted over the years. So too has the factory's ability to track them. In the early days when there were relatively few R22s about, the factory were able to keep track of all accidents. With the proliferation of R22s all over the world in the late 1980s it became very difficult. Some accidents were never even reported. Today, the factory only tracks those accidents investigated by the NTSB, the National Transportation Safety Board.

Early accidents in the R22 often took place while a student was under instruction, possibly because instructors were ex-military men who were used to big helicopters, not the light, sensitive R22. Robinson addressed this situation by creating its Safety Program which was aimed initially at Flight Instructors.

Fatal accidents before instigation of the factory Safety Program showed the following pattern:

Student Solos	36%
Dual Instruction	21%
Self-fly Hire	14%
Recreational	14%
Ferry from factory	14%

Statistics on fatal accidents after the Robinson Safety Course began showed a very different pattern:

Recreational	60%
Self-fly Hire	19%
Dual Instruction	12%
Student Solo	7%
Ferry from factory	2%

Based on the above it would seem fair to infer that students were soloing too early, and that instructors needed more training in the R22. The factory addressed the issue of customers having accidents when returning home after collecting their new helicopter by setting strict pilot and route requirements.

By the 1990s the pattern was changing. Five years into the 21st century the four major causes of accidents were respectively:
1. **W**ire strikes
2. **W**eather
3. **Low** rpm rotor stall
4. **Low** gravity push-overs
Or, to aid memory, the **two W's** and the **two Lows.**

If you look at the R22 Pilot's Operating Handbook, these hazards are flagged up in the Safety Notices:

wire	SN-16	Power lines are deadly
weather	SN-18	Loss of visibility can be fatal
weather	SN-26	Night flight plus bad weather
weather	SN-32	High winds or turbulence
low rpm	SN-10	Fatal accidents by low rpm rotor

low rpm   SN-24   Low rpm rotor stall can be fatal

low gravity SN-11   Low-G pushovers extreme danger

In addition to reading the above and listening to training instructors, why not also take instruction from the world experts on Robinson Helicopters: attend the Robinson Helicopter Safety Course at the Robinson factory in Torrance, California.

The course runs for four days and you won't be disappointed. The place, the people and the prep are all excellent. Factual information on the course is available on the Robinson web site at www.robinsonheli.com.

The place is of course Los Angeles. Torrance is only about 15 miles south of LAX. So if your flight arrives at midnight, the drive to the factory will only take 20 minutes. However, if it arrives during the rush hour, best allow 2 hours. There is the scenic route down Pacific Coast Highway, or join one of the many lanes on the Harbor Freeway. Either way, turn off Pacific Coast Highway at the traffic lights at Robinson Way and the factory presents itself.

The main drive leading to the glass, steel and cast concrete administration building is flanked by car parks for over 1000 employees. There is a bus service along Pacific Coast Highway, but the motorcar is still the preferred mode of transport in California.

Below: Viewed from across the airport, the Robinson buildings take up most of the west side. The low hills of Palos Verdes are in the background, with the Pacific Ocean just beyond. This photo was taken on a quiet Sunday morning. During the Safety Course the airport is teeming with Robinson 22s and 44s.

The size of the factory is surprising. Somehow because Robinson's is a privately owned company one tends to think of it as a modest family business. It is not. It is big business. Glistening white buildings flank a beautiful blue glass entrance foyer with row upon row of car parks for Robinson's many employees. Indeed the Robinson factory dominates the airfield.

The Safety Course includes a factory tour. Factory? It's more like a private clinic. A controlled environment of spotless pathways, separate work areas, and enclosed computer assisted equipment. Which is just as you would wish it to be since you are trusting your life to the quality of R22 construction every time you fly.
Alloy castings, wiring looms, tail booms, new shells with new kit, old shells for refits, crates from Lycoming, instruments for homing, testing machines and vending machines, are all on display as you make your way. Photography is not allowed in the working part of the factory itself, but visitors are free to photograph the finished helicopters awaiting delivery or collection in the hangar.

The course includes flight instruction of an hour or more in an R22 or 44. A number of instructors are brought in for the flying portion of the course which, when I attended, stretched over three days, Wednesday, Thursday and Friday, in order to accommodate everyone. The course was opened by Frank Robinson himself. He said that overall accidents are down except for R22 practice autorotations. He would like to promote the R44 for practice autos with its greater rotor inertia and gentler glide slope.

Regarding the R44 he expressed his dismay that pilots set off in them at night and in poor weather for a cross-country flight. Not only was this "really poor judgement," under some conditions it could be "absolute suicide." "Helicopters can be one of the safest modes of transport," Frank said, but pilots must take seriously their position of Pilot in Command.

39

In so many of the accidents that he has investigated he found that the pilot only needed a little more patience, caution and effort to have stayed out of trouble.

Listening to Frank Robinson it is obvious that he is a helicopter enthusiast, but this does not cloud his critical judgement regarding their safe use. Nor are accidents mere statistics. He wants you to have a long happy life flying Robinson helicopters, and the aim of the Safety Course is to ensure that you do.

He also spoke briefly about the development work on the "R55" or "R66." As the name implies this would be a 5 or 6 seat Robinson with, of necessity, a more powerful engine. Possibilities are a diesel engine, this would probably be too heavy, a turbocharged six cylinder piston engine, or most probably a turbine. Frank said that the new aircraft "may happen," but not for some time yet. He then handed over to Tim Tucker, the Robinson Safety Instructor.

I won't bother to list Tim Tucker's considerable qualifications and experience. On paper these lose their impact. During the three days in the classroom Tim never had to refer to notes. He was not simply repeating information that he had read somewhere: he knew what he was talking about from personal experience. And he was extraordinarily frank about himself and the company, not feeling the need to put a spin on things in order to make himself or the company always look exemplary. He was not above relating embarrassing things he'd done if it helped to illustrate a point regarding safety. At the same time he does not suffer fools gladly so it is best to pay attention during the course.

Attending the Robinson Safety course is a singularly sufficient reason to visit Los Angeles. But if you have time, there are other helicopter related things to do. For example there is the annual Edwards Air Force Base Open House.

Edwards is located 100 miles northeast of Los Angeles in the Mojave Desert, famous for Joshua trees and, well, Joshua trees. It takes in 44 square miles of unique dry lake bed which is naturally smooth, hard and level, perfect for long, long runways. The dry lake bed of hardened clay provides an additional 9,000 feet / 2743 metres of effective runway overrun. Manston Airport in Kent, formerly RAF Manston, is famous for its long runway of 2752 metres. You would have thought the 4572 metres of main concrete runway at Edwards would be sufficient, but perhaps not when flying experimental aircraft or returning from space. You may have seen the space shuttle landing at Edwards when Florida was overcast. Most of the training for space flight took place at Edwards.

On view will be US military helicopters such as the Blackhawk, CH-46 Sea Knight, and up-rated Huey. Examining these complex machines close up and sitting in the cockpit surrounded by bank after bank of instruments makes you feel grateful for the relative simplicity of the R22.

As well as static displays there are aerial displays from new fighter jets. On the day I visited, Chuck Yeager flew his World War II Mustang alongside a new F/A-22 Raptor. Perhaps one day in the future old men will come to gaze upon the Raptor as the epitome of romantic fighter aircraft of old. Perhaps.

Whatever debate might develop about the relative achievements of the two aircraft, one thing is for certain about the pilots. No one is ever likely to surpass Chuck Yeager's achievements: World War II ace pilot, test pilot, the first human to travel faster than sound. It's just a shame that the military never transferred him to helicopters!

Chuck Yeager flew his North American P-51 Mustang, above,

into Edwards Air Force Base for the Open House. The large air scoop placed aft and under the cockpit is unmistakably Mustang. Now into his 80's, General Yeager, left, remains fit and is still enthusiastic about flying. Seeing him at the controls of a World War II fighter was the highlight of the show for many.

The front of the Sikorsky CH53 Sea Stallion looks like a diesel locomotive …with 7 rotor blades. The tilt-rotor Osprey, below, should combine the best of fixed wing and helicopter flight. Notwithstanding that it first flew in 1989, it has not really taken off.

Frank Robinson Interview

> Genius is the ability to put into effect what is
> on your mind.
>
> F. Scott Fitzgerald

HB: How did all this happen?

FR: Not too many years ago it was really small. It was really in my house up in a tract in PV [Palos Verdes—a leafy suburb next to Torrance]. Then, there was a tin hangar located about where this building is actually. From there we went to a building over on Crenshaw and Sky Park Drive. We actually went into production and produced quite a few helicopters over there. And then designed and built this building in the summer of '94.

HB: Was it when you got financial backing from Gus Lefiell that you were able to embark on your R22 company?

FR: I'd already made that decision, but he and I had become friends before that. He wanted to build a home-built helicopter and he wanted to hire a consultant who knew a lot about helicopters to produce a design that he was going to build. He was very successful; he had a company that manufactured products for Boeing and others. He had asked different people he knew from Northrop and other companies that he'd done business with, and one of the engineers there recommended me because of my background in helicopters. So he contacted me and that's how we got to know each other.

Totally separate from that I had reached the point in my own life when I had tried to start a company. I was never able to get the thing off the ground and get moving with it. I had people working in my house in Fort Worth, Texas when I worked for Bell. We tried to get financing from different people in Fort Worth. It's just that we were not successful in doing it.

I had tried before when I was in Florida and had tried when I worked for McCulloch. McCulloch was a real good old boy, very successful, very wealthy. I knew him quite well. I worked for him four and a half years I think.

We tested a gyrodyne and I was the project engineer on it. But I tried real hard to get him interested in the little helicopter that I had designed. He didn't want to go that way. He already had the McCulloch helicopter which was a tandem helicopter. The military had evaluated it. It had kind of gone by the wayside.

He wanted me to keep working on this idea I had for a gyroplane, a kind of half helicopter, half gyroplane. I had some patent rights and so forth for it. But I got impatient and was going to leave. To get me to stay for another year or whatever he paid for me to get my helicopter rating. He was a good person. That was back in the early sixties.

After I left McCulloch I went to Kaman up in Connecticut, and from Kaman I went to Bell in Fort Worth, Texas. Then from Bell I went to Hughes.

It was when I was at Hughes that I was 43 years old. I knew that if I didn't try to do my own thing then there was no way that I was ever going to do it. And I decided that it was now or never.

So I bought some property. I was going to build a house that I had designed with a really large garage space. I thought if I could get some outside financing I could complete the design of the helicopter and fabricate a prototype there. It did not turn out that way.

In the meantime I had given in my notice at Hughes and quit. In one of my meetings with Gus Lefiell I told him what I was going to do. I was already committed to it. He was really interested and wanted to know if he could join me in it. I knew he had a lot of money, so I didn't turn it down. So we worked out a very fair written agreement drawn up by his lawyer and started the company. That is how I started.

HB: Did you employ a designer for the R22?
FR: I designed the aircraft myself. I had a little bit of help in certain areas. One of the draftsmen I had was quite good and he did a lot of sheet metal work and was quite good at it in the design.
The way I worked in those days was quite different from the way I work now. I used blue cross-hatch paper and I could come up with a design for anything from the gearbox to the rotor blade, whatever, on that paper and define everything on it real fast. Then I would give it to one of the draftsmen to go ahead and make the detailed drawings. That system worked real good.

I was able to design pretty much all of it. A little bit of the sheet metal stuff Joe did the original design, but not very much. I had my ideas formulated before I ever started the company. I'd been working on them for years and years.

When I worked for McCulloch, particularly, I had a very free hand and worked on whatever I wanted to work on. I developed a lot of the ideas when I was working at McCulloch. But it had actually started way back when I first got out of college and when I was in college.

Out of college I went directly to Cessna and worked on the Cessna helicopter. At home I had my own little basement workshop and spent all my money on tools, welding equipment, engine lathes and all that kind of stuff. So I'd done a lot of the design work before I started as a company. I had worked on a lot of the ideas and actually had built different models and tested them in my basement workshop.

I dragged those tools around the country as I moved to work for different companies. I have to laugh because there are still some of those things here in this company still in use. The foot shear that I bought for shearing sheet metal is still right here still being used the last time I saw it. The drill press that I bought is still out there still being used. And the little engine lathe that I bought which is a little Atlas engine lathe is still being used in the experimental. I had acetylene welding equipment that I used a lot, but I lost track of it. I had my own little rivet gun that I bought when I was at Cessna, a little 2X Chicago. Then I did a lot of work with fibreglass. There are different ways of making fibreglass. I did a lot of the experimenting over those years. It was sixteen years that I was working at other companies.

HB: You formed the company in 1973 and flew the prototype in 1975?
FR: August of '75. Yes.

HB: You flew it yourself.
FR: Oh yes, sure.

HB: Were you thinking to yourself, is it actually going to work properly?
FR: Oh I knew that it was going to work! [laughter] I had a lot of experience by then. I was very fortunate in that right from the very beginning I would not accept any specialization. I did not want to be a stress engineer, or design engineer and so on. I wanted to be proficient in all areas, and I was able to get away with that. Very often in the various companies I worked for I was the only engineer that had that privilege.

That was really good because it gave me an opportunity to become familiar with manufacturing. I did a lot of flight test work, I also did a lot of design and stress analysis. As a result of those sixteen years I did have a very broad background. And during the latter part of those years because I had a broad background I was used in those various companies as a kind of problem solver.

By the time I started this company I had a very good background so I was able to move quite rapidly in designing the R22. I knew what it was going to be like before I ever started the company. I had a lot of the ideas already in my head and then came up with additional ideas.

At the big companies they'll design a new aircraft and they'll build a test bed and they'll go through a whole bunch of pre-tests and ground tests and all sorts of things. I did not have the money to do all that. I designed the original R22 as a production helicopter right from the beginning.

I worked it out and analysed everything as I went along. I did stress analysis and also aerodynamics because I had both a mechanical engineering and aeronautical background. So when we rolled that R22 down to the west end of the field to try it, I had a whole list of different things that were untested at that point. The clutch engagement system, the flexible couplings, the tail rotor, none of it had been tested, but it had all been designed based on experience and analysis.

So we fired it up and ran up the rotor and everything worked okay. We had blocks on the control systems so it couldn't go anywhere. We flight tracked the blades and they came into reasonable track pretty easily. Everything seemed to work pretty good. I just went through everything really fast. What would have taken—at Bell or some other company—weeks or even months of testing and evaluating and all this sort of thing. By noon I was through all of it.

Finally I couldn't think of anything else that I needed to test. So I told the guys to pull the blocks out of the control systems. It felt alright. It wasn't going crazy. So I told everybody to get back and clear the area.

I went ahead and lifted it off. It flew just fine. I made a number of flights that afternoon hovering and just air taxiing flights; no up and away flights at that point. Everything worked. It didn't all work as well as I wanted it to. There was some feedback in the controls and things like that, but those were details to work out.

It had a centrifugal clutch I'd designed, but it was heavy and it gave me some trouble on the early flights although it did actually work pretty good. It had a nice safe easy engagement. You did not have to worry about overspeed or anything, but I decided I could do a belt tensioning engagement instead that would be a lot lighter.

I designed the actuator that we have in the R22 now that automatically engages it. That was kind of fun designing that. I got to use a principle that I wanted to use, but had not found an application for: the principle of a collapsed column.

A collapsed column is fairly unique because it has a zero spring rate. I wanted to take advantage of that and here I had an opportunity to, finally, for something that I could use that principle in. It worked and we've used it ever since.

Other helicopters had belt drives, but in this case it was different in that it raised and lowered the upper sheave to engage the rotor. It has to tension that. The tension takes a lot of force. You're talking about a couple thousand pounds of force. So the design I came up with would produce that high tension. It would do it slow enough so it wouldn't kill the engine as it engages it, and would also sense the compression load in the actuator so that it would turn it off when it reached the prescribed tension in the belts.

The way it works out, it does that and also if the belts stretch a little bit and the tension falls off, it will turn itself back on, re-tension the belt and shut itself off again. That is what it is doing when the clutch light comes on and goes back off again in flight.

So they work pretty good. It allowed me to use an optimum loading of the Vee belts so the calculated life would be considerably greater than if you tried to do it with fixed pulleys.

Anyhow, that's the story of how the original R22 was done.

HB: So it was four years later that you got type certification for it from the FAA?
FR: We did the first flight in 1975 and finally got type certification in March of '79 I think.

HB: Were you getting impatient to start marketing it?
FR: That whole time I spent an immoderate amount of time just raising money. It was so difficult! I was absolutely sure that once I had a prototype that flew, and flew reasonably well, that I would have no trouble getting investors. Not true at all.

I had so many venture capitalists come out, and I'd give them all a demonstration of the helicopter. A lot of them were from big companies, they all have venture capital departments. The venture capitalist is probably the worst way in the world to raise money. Number one, he wants to get his return in no more than two or three years. Number two, he expects to get 30 to 35% return on that investment.

I could not in any way have a business plan that showed getting that money back in less than five years. Getting it back in five years would be amazing; certainly not in two or three. There is no way that you can build a company if you are servicing a debt at that rate of interest. So finally I used all sorts of other ways to raise money.

I had one lucky break. I called the West Coast editor for Aviation Weekly, a prestigious magazine with a wide circulation throughout the world. I told him about the little helicopter that I'd built and he came out and I gave him a really good demonstration in it. I could fly pretty good by then. He was really intrigued by it and he wrote quite a long article in Aviation Week, a really extensive article.

All the other magazines read each other's magazines. They started contacting me wanting to write articles on this little helicopter. So I got a lot of really good free publicity. A lot of people contacted me wanting to buy one or be a dealer for them. So I set up a marketing plan which involved dealers, and I took deposits.

I did not take deposits like some promoters have over the years. I knew about flaky promoters and I wanted to be sure I didn't get into that category. So when I started taking deposits I made absolutely sure I always told the truth and didn't exaggerate anything. I said that the money collected on the deposits would be put in a separate bank account and would only be used to buy production parts and materials for producing the helicopters. It would not be used for development or experimental work. That was really good because I could also use it to buy parts and materials for tests that had to be conducted like the fatigue tests because these were all production parts.

We had a very small deposit required, something like three hundred dollars, but it was a non-refundable deposit. Except you could ask for a refund at any time for any reason and get 50%

back. So it constituted a real order. And for the dealerships the deposit requirement was considerably higher. So we were able to show to banks or other lenders that we had quite a large number of orders all of which had a non-refundable deposit put down. Everything was out in the open.

That was very helpful in getting some debt capital, although even then without having collateral to put up it was difficult. So I did not really get very much bank money. I did for buying some machinery because they knew there was collateral behind it. But the deposits themselves added quite a bit of money, and let's see.... There were just a whole bunch of other ways that I had to use.

I sold some stock in the company. I didn't want to sell too much because I didn't want to start losing control. I concentrated more on deposits on the aircraft. Then two different times sold the right to negotiate for a production license in a foreign country. I did that for a group in Italy and later for a group in Japan. Those were profitable deals. Then I brought in large outside investors. Some of the employees also bought some of the stock. And I sold stock to a doctor who had just made a lot of money. He invested a few hundred thousand and my original partner had by that time invested a couple hundred thousand.

HB: How many employees did you have then?
FR: Before production, during development it varied anywhere from just two or three up to six or seven.

HB: So you had to meet all their salaries during that period?
FR: Yes, except some or most of the employees were taking part of their salary first in stock, and then equity in a production helicopter. Whatever they took in equity in a production helicopter that was going to be doubled when they cashed it in on the helicopter. So we gave them a two to one return. I was very careful to always honour all of those agreements. And I did. So there

were just a whole bunch of different things I did to raise money.

It took an awful lot of money to put it into production. We had to bootstrap our way through, but I did have those two large outside investors, my original partner and the doctor.

HB: Did you eventually buy them out?
FR: Yes. My partner Gus died and we had in our original agreement if either of us died the other could buy out his stock at par value and have ten years to pay it off. So I exercised that clause when he died. Then we brought in one large outside investor. Big money people.

That was right after the R22 had gone into production, but we had just flatly run out of money, and had some problems to solve and I had to lay everybody off. I was really destitute when I brought them in.

HB: You found them? You went to them?
FR: Indirectly. I had become friends with the president of a big company who was a helicopter nut. I called him in New York and told him my plight. He personally did not have the million or two to bale me out, but he did know who did have that kind of money and could raise whatever money they needed to, very, very fast. So he put me in contact with them and I invited them out. They spent a few hours taking a walk through and said, alright, we'll take a couple million of that, and they did. They were the largest outside investor.

HB: After that you were financially okay.
FR: No. There started to be lawsuits and all sorts of problems. In subsequent years we were able to meet the payroll, but it was a real challenge every Friday to get that damn payroll. Everybody became discouraged because there didn't seem to be any light at the end of the tunnel. Primarily because of the lawsuits, wrongful

death lawsuits, people having accidents.

Prior to my partner's death, of the four main investors or owners we each owned 23% of the company. One of those was myself. I had my stock in exchange for my patent rights and ideas. Then there was my original partner Gus. He owned 23% and the doctor had 23% and the other family had 23% and the remaining percentage was owned by a number of the employees.

When my partner died and I exercised my right to his stock that gave me 46%. The 46% plus the about 6% that the employees owned gave me over 51%, so I then had control. The board meetings up to that point were [laughter] very, very bad because the outsiders had totally different interests than the insiders. I never had any problems with the employees. They always voted with me. We saw things the same way. The outside investors didn't.

When I got control of it the company was still not doing well at all. It had all those lawsuits and everything, and one by one the investors wanted out. First the doc got out. He took a little bit of a loss, not a bad loss, to get out. I was able to raise outside money to buy him out. I made deals on helicopters and all sorts of different ways to raise the money.

The family from New York were still in. They were okay. I liked them. They were real straightforward. They were tough and they let me know right up front they could put me under anytime. I said: "I realize that and understand that very clearly, but that isn't going to be to your advantage and it's sure as hell not going to be to my advantage." So that wasn't going to happen.

Finally at a certain point things were just not looking any better. Several more years had passed so when they were disappointed with a quarterly report I said, "Do you want to stay in or would you really rather get out?" He said: "To be honest, Frank, we'd really rather get out." He wanted me to make him an offer. I said that I can't do that because what I would have to offer would be based on what I think I can raise and that would be an insult as it is no where near what you have in. "Okay, don't worry about it being an insult. Just go ahead and come up with something."

I pinned him down just a little bit as to what would be the minimum he would be able to consider. I went ahead and made that offer and he gave me 30 days to raise it or something like that. True to his word, I had that amount by such and such a date and it was a done deal. I think that is when I sold the negotiating rights to other countries and things like that. I was able to raise quite a bit. I think insurance was involved in one of them. Anyhow, I was able to put together the money and bought out that outside investor.

As time went by the company gradually began to turn around. Gradually it started to actually make a little bit of money. Over a period of years I was able to buy out the employee stock holders. I made sure that all of them got a good return on their investment. Eventually I got to where I had 100% of the stock, and it's been that way ever since. The company has done fine.

HB: Please could I just ask you about the R22 cyclic? It is so unique. How did that come about?
FR: It was a way to solve several problems. One of the problems is that a helicopter as small and light as the R22 you worry about control sensitivity particularly the lateral control because the roll inertia of that helicopter is so small compared to a large helicopter and you are getting all of your control power by the height of the rotor above the CG. It's very difficult to not have a real sensitive lateral control.

The easiest way or most direct way to reduce that sensitivity is to increase the control travel. Suppose I had a stick here on the floor [demonstrating]. That's my maximum travel. So I came up with that design because it solved several problems. One, it greatly simplified the control mechanism. You don't have all that interconnecting linkage, just the one centre thing. And by having this T bar cyclic or whatever you want to call it, it allowed me, or the pilot, to go across his knees so that he could get a full 14 inches of lateral stick travel which you would never get with one between your knees.

Another important advantage is that it made getting in and out of the R22 much easier. Particularly for a girl with a skirt on you don't have to climb over a cyclic stick to get in and out. And I designed it as a personal helicopter.

HB: Channel 5 in the UK televised a program called "The World's Greatest Helicopters." The R22 was voted second greatest and the Huey came in first.
FR: The Bell Huey? It's a good helicopter.

HB: But for most people the R22 will always be number 1. The Huey has an illustrious image, but most of us will never fly one.
FR: That's right. It's not a personal helicopter. I designed the R22 purely as a personal helicopter, the type of helicopter that I would want to buy and own myself. That was the criteria that I used for it. It had to be simple, easy to maintain, efficient. Those type of things.

Since I already knew how to fly a helicopter I didn't design it to be the easiest helicopter in the world to fly. It is not. It has rather quick controls and a quickness about it.

HB: Some instructors say that if you can fly an R22 you can fly anything.

FR: I've heard that a lot. And basically it's true, because the quickness of it means that if you get used to the R22 you're always going to be ahead of the other helicopters. You anticipate things very quickly. People at Bell used to tell me any number of different times: "You know the pilots that come here to get checked out in the Bell products that have learned in an R22 can fly better than the pilots that learned in a Bell." [laughter].

HB: It's kind of a curious compliment isn't it? It's a difficult helicopter to fly, but...
FR: It teaches you good habits. You have to have good habits or you are going to get hurt. The R22 is fast for a small light helicopter compared to the 47 [Bell] and a lot of the older ones.

HB: Did you initially expect it was going to be so popular as a trainer?
FR: I misjudged that. I thought that the flight schools already had their 47s and their Hillers and Brantlys and others. I just did not recognise that as the potential market that it would be. I thought that the only people who would be taking training in it would be the customers that bought it. But I was wrong. It became extremely popular very, very rapidly in flight schools all over the world.

HB: There must be an R22 in flight somewhere 24 hours a day. You can go to bed at night thinking my helicopter is flying....
FR: [Laughter] You don't get a good night's sleep anytime because there is always somebody out there flying one! [laughter].

FR: Well, that's about it.
HB: Thanks very much.

Frank Robinson

Looking good and enjoying incredible worldwide success, Frank Robinson has received virtually every major award the industry has to offer, yet remains remarkably modest about his achievements and the pleasure his helicopter has given to so many.

The three helicopters referred to by Frank Robinson that were used for pilot training at the time that the R22 came out were the Hiller, Brantly and the Bell 47. The Hiller above is a UH-12C from 1958. The Brantly below according to the lettering on it is a B-2B and looks little changed from the first certificated model B-2 of 1959.

The Bell 47 has the distinction of being the first commercial helicopter to be awarded a Type Approval Certificate. That was in 1946. Coincidentally, at about the same time, in 1947 Bell produced the first airplane to fly faster than sound when Chuck Yeager flew the Bell X-1 at Mach 1.06, 45,000 feet above Edwards Air Force Base. It just shows how far behind helicopters were in development compared with fixed wing aircraft.

Thousands of Bell 47s were built, mostly for military use. Fitted with external stretcher carriers their use in the Korean War was popularised by the TV series, M*A*S*H. Performance of the 47 is similar to the R22 in terms of maximum and cruising speeds, but the aircraft itself is heavier and it carries a much heavier load. Its vertically mounted 6 cylinder Lycoming engine (later models) would as a trainer burn up a lot more fuel than the R22.

The bright paintwork on the above 47 shows off the design of the helicopter much more effectively than does military olive drab.

Wherever you fly, there will probably be an assortment of Robinson R22 models. Above: a Beta, a Beta Mariner and a silver Beta II. Below: three versions of the Beta II. Each will have its own idiosyncrasies, but all will be typically challenging and entertaining.

Training school helicopters are usually available for self-fly hire. Before allowing someone to fly away in one of their R22s they will probably first want to confirm the pilot's competence. They will of course charge for this assessment flight with one of their instructors. There may also be a requirement to sign a deed of indemnity, which is a promise to pay for any claims or damage to the helicopter whilst in the hirer's custody.

Notwithstanding this precaution, there are ways to harm the helicopter that are not immediately apparent. Failure to report accidents such as over-speeds could also endanger subsequent users. So it is quite important that the pilot at the controls understands this and flies responsibly.

Buy or Borrow

Why buy a cow if you only require a regular supply of milk?

Old Adage

To own a cow, there is the expense of buying the cow in the first place. Then there is feeding it, keeping it somewhere, looking after its health and worrying it could have an accident and die. So you may wish to insure it and that is another expense. And one day of course, at the end of all this, it will die of old age anyway. So what's the point?

Maybe ever since you were little you wanted a cow of your own. Maybe you like being around cows and looking after them. Maybe you want to be sure of having milk whenever you wish. Maybe you know of somewhere to keep it and someone who will sell the extra milk for you.

Clearly there are valid views on both sides of this polemic. So let's examine them in detail, and for the sake of argument let's talk about helicopters instead of cows.

The R22 is one of the cheapest helicopters to buy. You can buy one for less than the price of a Ferrari Maranello or Porsche GT2. Looking around, quite a few people seem to own one of those cars. So quite a few people could own an R22. But, with an aircraft you won't do 5,000 miles between services. Nor will you have any choice in the matter. With a car you can choose to ignore maintenance; with an aircraft maintenance is dictated by law. And when it comes to maintaining an aircraft, it is going to be a long way from cheap.

Just like cars, if you purchase second hand you will want a pre-purchase inspection by a qualified person and a test flight. Alternatively buy new and receive a two year factory warranty. Refinements such as additional instruments, night lights, and metallic paintwork will increase the price. But if all you are after is an R22 to call your own, simply buy the cheaper one with only the basics. You can always add on later, and portable GPS are much less expensive than built-in, and easier to upgrade.

Having made your purchase, where do you keep it? If you are fortunate in having a large suitable plot with garage and understanding neighbours you may keep it at home. Alternatively you can pay for parking or hangar space at a local airport. Whichever you choose, it is best to keep it indoors. The expense will repay itself in a tamper-free, cleaner, drier, less faded and weather worn machine. And, most importantly, all of the above will make it a safer aircraft.

When shopping for an airport to hangar your R22 look for one with a Robinson Agency or Service Centre on site. This will make life much easier and save a lot of ferrying. For example, if your helicopter has to be flown somewhere else for service, you will have to pay for the fuel to get there and back, and time will be taken off the Datcon to no good purpose. If the weather is poor, it may not be possible to fly it there. Also, if it should develop a fault which precludes it being flown for service, it will be grounded until a mechanic is able to drive out to repair it. Whereas if it is already on site it can be serviced regardless of the weather, and will be available immediately the weather improves.

But before settling on a maintenance organization to place it with, ask around about them. Some are excellent, and some are less than excellent. The latter can waste your time and money. They may meet the minimum requirements for your R22, after all there are laws covering aircraft maintenance, but there is a significant difference between a mediocre and a good job. There is doing a job, and there is being interested in what you do and taking pride in it. Note what Kurt Robinson has to say about maintenance in chapter seven.

Unless you are entirely free of other commitments and are able to fly every day if you wish, you will probably not put very many hours on your R22 in a year. You may find that service intervals are determined by calendar dates rather than hours flown, i.e. the date for its 100 hour service comes up before it has actually flown another 100 hours, which is a bit of a waste.

To keep it in regular use you could lease it to a helicopter training school. This will generate an income to offset your expenses. On the other hand, it will be flown by learners who are likely to make mistakes. It could suffer an engine over-speed or rotor over-speed, a hard landing or even a roll-over. End of your pride and joy! And even though you have it insured, the deductible amount on any claim is substantial, and you will be out of pocket for this shortfall.

Looked at purely from an economic point of view you need to calculate your likely annual flying hours, multiplied by the hourly hire rate. Then set that against the cost of ownership: purchase price, maintenance, both planned and unplanned (to be sure, there will be some unplanned, and whatever amount you think you should set aside for this, double it), insurance, hangarage, fuel, depreciation and so on. If the two sums are fairly close, then you will have to consider other factors. Do you want all the paperwork of ownership? Are you relaxed about other people flying your ship? Or is your personality more suited to pay-as-you-go, with no worries?

There are many advantages to simply hiring a helicopter by the hour. You can hire from any airport you like. Once you have flown with one of their instructors and they are satisfied that you are safe, you may ring up and book an R22 whenever you like. So you are able to explore different areas of the country instead of always flying out of the same place. If one airfield is prone to unpredictable weather, fly somewhere else. You will also be in a position to compare various R22s, and of course no two are exactly alike. At the end of the flight you can shut the door and walk away, care free.

Whatever you decide to do, it does not have to be permanent. If you choose to buy, you may discover that the correct answer to the question:
"How do you make a million in the helicopter business?"
is indeed:
"Start out with two million."

But, if you purchase an R22 and subsequently decide that ownership is not for you, you can always sell it later. They hold their value fairly well and like a cheap and cheerful compact car there will always be a demand for them. And notwithstanding the 25 plus years they have been in production there is not that much difference between the years. The later ones may have more refinements such as the vertical compass and trigger radio, but the earlier 0-320 engine models are easier on fuel.

Owning or renting is really just a case of - to return to our opening analogy - different ways of getting the milk that you require. The main thing is to get out and enjoy your milk, whether it comes from your own cow or someone else's.

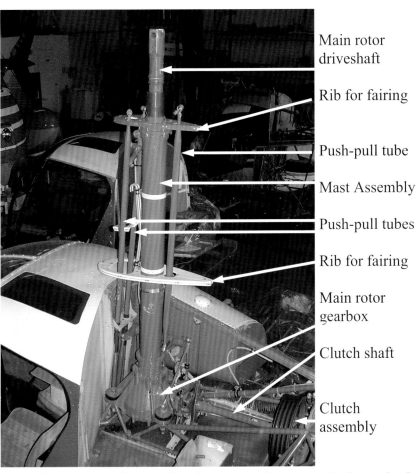

Main rotor driveshaft

Rib for fairing

Push-pull tube

Mast Assembly

Push-pull tubes

Rib for fairing

Main rotor gearbox

Clutch shaft

Clutch assembly

One of the perks of ownership is that you have permission to be in the hangar and can see R22s in pieces. With the main tank, rotor fairing and rear cowling off this R22 you get a better understanding of how it works.

The main rotor gearbox must be unequivocally in good order. It has a Telatemp temperature recorder strip next to the sight-gauge and a warning light for abnormally high temperatures, and a chip warning light which indicates metal particles in the gearbox. Ferrous particles as small as .13 inches long or .03 wide mean that the gearbox goes back to RHC for repair.

Accidents

Practice autorotations continue to be a primary cause of accidents in the R22 and R44. Each year many helicopters are destroyed practicing for the engine failure that very rarely occurs.

RHC Safety Notice SN-38

An R22 Instructor talks about the practice autorotation accident that occurred while training a student for his commercial license:

When you are doing autos you demand a lot of power at the end when you are trying to recover. The power came back, but it did not have enough power. So when I brought the power back in, I felt it didn't have full power. It was like: put-put-put-put. You hear the blades slowing down and then the horn came on.

I put the collective down again and full throttle up. We were at only 200 feet. So I went for air speed again, the rpm's, and flared. Unfortunately when we came down we had a little bit of tail wind I think, and the terrain wasn't even. So flare, put it down, and a bunch of grass caught my skid and we rolled over. Both skids touched level, but I saw the grass was high. At the end I thought, okay, great, everything went fine because I flared and it was looking so good, and then the next minute we were upside down. Everything happened so fast.

We do full down here [at the airport] all the time. The only difference here is we have the space to slide it. There [in a distant field] we had that little pivot point and that's all you need. If we'd come down on the tarmac runway no problem. Maybe a little bit of a hard landing, but no big deal.

When I landed I didn't realize it was so bad. You just walk away. Some workers in the field said: "How do you walk away from that?" Then I turned around and saw the helicopter in pieces. It was totalled. The student with me was half a mile away!
"You okay?" I said.
"Yah, now I've calmed down."

The engine was removed and tested with National Transportation Safety Board and FAA oversight. The NTSB determined the probable cause of this accident as:
The partial loss of engine power due to low cylinder compression during recovery from a practice autorotation resulting in a hard landing and damage to the helicopter.

The student I was flying with almost quit. After three days I finally got him to do an auto again. He took his check ride and went home with his commercial.

Rodrigo Peñaranda,   Lantana, Florida

Any helicopter may suffer a mechanical failure or partial failure which may lead to damage to the helicopter. Randy Rowles talks about his experience with autorotations:

I've had several engine malfunctions. One resulted in an actual accident in an R22. I am still a big believer in the aircraft even though it happened. It wasn't my fault. It was a mechanical malfunction. The safety mechanisms that were designed for the aircraft worked very well. That's why neither occupant of the aircraft in a relatively devastating crash was really injured at all. So I'm a believer in the aircraft.

You can be within the altitude, airspeed combinations to make safe autorotations, but if the surface texture is not appropriate it does not allow you to land. We were over soft terrain, and when it hit the ground the left skid dug into the ground. That's just the way it is.

Training we use grass areas in the centre of the airport and places like that. But, when you have an actual emergency the soft ground can catch a skid and cause the aircraft to roll over. The design features are not to save the aircraft, the design features are to save the occupants, and it worked very well.

High vertical speed accidents in R22s are very common. In this particular situation the National Transportation Safety Board had an opinion of the R22 and they weren't going to investigate it. They told me on the phone that it sounded like another high vertical speed accident in an R22. I told them that I didn't agree with that. They started asking about my background. They found that I'm not a 200 or 500 hour helicopter pilot, but an 8000 hour helicopter pilot with a lot of experience in R22s. They then stood up and listened to what I had to say about what happened.

The NTSB report states:
<u>Following recovery of the helicopter, the engine was started and operated in the airframe with no discrepancies noted. The engine was then removed from the helicopter, placed in a test cell and operated with a test club installed. The engine was started and only operated to approximately 2,550 rpm instead of 2,700 rpm. Low differential compression (5 psi) of the No. 3 cylinder was noted when testing using 80 psi.</u>

I found through this experience that I think a lot of the situations that happen to Robinson's are due to the fact that you have lower time, lower experience pilots flying these aircraft and sometimes they can get themselves into trouble. The aircraft itself you wear like a glove. It's very easy to get over-confident in this aircraft. So it is really important that flight schools and owners of flight

79

schools and chief pilots maintain control of the manoeuvres that are done, and where they are done. You want to allow instructors the greatest opportunity of success if they do have a malfunction.

Out of the four parts of an autorotation: the entry, the glide, the flare, and the landing, the three that have to be consistent are the entry, glide and flare. In the landing phase you are completely dependent upon what is underneath you at the time.

We have changed our procedures since we had our accident. We are only doing practice autorotations over areas that we know in the event of an engine failure we can get it on the ground safely, on the runway, to give the instructor that added benefit.

It happens in any helicopter. I've had to autorotate a Jet Ranger twice. I wasn't in the right place in one, but both were without incident just because the aircraft characteristics are so different from a Robinson. If I'd been in a Robinson I would probably have broken the aircraft, especially in one of them. But that goes back to: Why would I be in a Robinson doing that mission? The mission has to have the proper aircraft. Safety should be the primary limitation.

Look at the US military. They break aircraft a lot, but we don't use those statistics because it's in the military. You could take a Bell Jet Ranger, which is the safest single engine aircraft in the world, and put it into a training environment and the accident rate would go up. You are teaching less experienced pilots how to fly. That inherently is a risky business. So your accident and incident rate would increase.

If the Robinson were not doing any training whatsoever and all they were doing is personal transport from A to B we wouldn't have the autorotation accidents because they wouldn't be in that environment.   Randy Rowles, Fort Worth, Texas

80

Consider the following NTSB report as an example of low time, low experience pilots getting themselves into trouble in R22s.

NTSB Identification: ATL00LA059
Aircraft: Robinson R22 Beta
Injuries: 2 uninjured

The student pilot planned a cross-country flight from Ft. Lauderdale to Pahokee, Florida, then to Stuart, Florida, with a final destination of Ft. Lauderdale. However, according to the Martin County Sheriff's Department, the pilot diverted to the Martin County Treatment Center in Indiantown, Florida. While hovering over the facility's recreation yard, he picked up a passenger who was an inmate at the center. During initial climb following takeoff, the helicopter struck a tree, then collided with the ground in a citrus grove 100 yards from the facility's perimeter.

The Martin County Treatment Center is not your average treatment centre. It is in fact linked with the Martin County Correctional Institution (prison) which has armed guards. The Treatment Center is a secure separate facility on the same site. It too has fencing topped with razor wire, but there are Therapeutic Assistants instead of armed guards. Still, it is not the ideal site for a student pilot to attempt a confined area landing and takeoff. Especially after taking on the added weight of what the NTSB refer to as a "passenger." (How is that for being impeccably disinterested). And at one o'clock on a June afternoon with the temperature in the 30s Centigrade, the Lycoming 0-320 engine will not have a lot of power to spare.

Nevertheless, having lifted over the razor wire and cleared the yard, you'd have thought that his immediate worries were over. Not so. He struck a tree, went into an uncontrolled descent, hit the ground and rolled over. The R22 was finished, but the occupants walked away, or more accurately, ran away. They were still only about 100 yards from the Centre and not much further from the Correctional Facility's armed guards.

The manhunt for them in the surrounding swampland lasted for two days. By the time they were found and arrested, they were probably not sorry to leave the habitat of snakes and alligators and get into clean, dry clothes, albeit prison issue, and eat a hot meal.

The ingenuous 25-year-old student pilot, who had no prior police record, entered a plea of *nolo contendere* to Reckless Operation of an Aircraft in violation of Florida Statute 860.13(1)(b). He was sentenced to 48 months in custody. Additionally, a condition of subsequent probation was a court order for $114,600 restitution for the ill-fated R22. His friend, on the other hand, who had prior felony convictions, was charged with Armed Escape While in Lawful Custody, and went away for a long time.

All of this was of course extraneous to the NTSB's investigation as to the cause of the accident. They determined the probable cause was:

The student pilot's failure to maintain altitude clearance during initial climb following takeoff during the commission of a crime, resulting in an in-flight collision with a tree.

There is a lesson here for all helicopter pilots. If you are collecting a friend in your helicopter, try to meet him somewhere with a proper helipad. And check first to make sure he is not in custody.

The Martin Correctional Institution outside Indiantown, Florida is surrounded by inhospitable scrub. Having said that, apart from the odd fence and tree, it is flat as a crêpe and not difficult as a navigation exercise. The ocean is just 12 miles due east. The Treatment Centre, below, has the same secure fencing, but is a separate facility on the same site.

Kurt Robinson Interview

They all laughed at Wilbur and his brother
When they said that man could fly
They told Marconi, wireless was a phoney
It's the same old cry...
Now they'll have to change their tune.

George and Ira Gershwin,
They All Laughed

HB: How old were you when your father was drawing plans for the R22?
KR: The first time I remember ever seeing any kind of a drawing on it specifically, in my memory, was when we were back in Texas when I was in the fifth grade. In the mid sixties, something like that.

HB: You must have been the envy of all your schoolmates if you had a dad who was into helicopters.
KR: [Laughter] No, not really. Particularly when we lived in Palos Verdes most of my friends' dads were engineers for various companies. My dad happened to work with a company that did helicopters, but I had other friends whose dads were working on satellites or other aircraft. There were a lot of engineers so it wasn't that big a deal. It was an engineering community. People tend to cluster together and at that time he was a helicopter engineer.

The impressive drop off, of course, was when he quit and started his own company. People would kind of cock an eye at you when you told them: "Well actually he is working on a project," we referred to it as a project then, "trying to design a little helicopter." People would look at you, not that they didn't believe you, but when you hear somebody say that they are going to try to do something, you don't know whether they are going to make it or not. But, it sounds like they are probably not going to so you don't want to say anything bad. I think that is the look most people would give me.

HB: Having grown up with helicopters in the family, did you want to go into the helicopter business too?
KR: I didn't really think about it. I know my father wanted me to be an engineer. It really wasn't my cup of tea, and at some point in college I came back to him and said that I actually prefer business and economics. I said that what would be really interesting for me would be to go to a company that was having difficulties and help straighten them out and turn them around.

When I got out of college I needed a couple more years to get my MBA. My dad said: "Why don't you come home? I am just trying to get this started and we are having some problems. Why don't you work with us?" So I did. Basically to earn money to go back to school.

It was at some point during those two years while I was working with my dad that it became obvious to me that that was what I was going to do. When I went back to get my MBA we were having a bunch of legal issues as every business does in the United States and my dad said to me: "I need an attorney a hell of a lot more than I need somebody with an MBA." So I decided to get both and that is what I went on to do.

HB: So you handle all the litigation that comes your way?
KR: Well actually I recruited another gentleman that I went to law school with. He is actually our head corporate attorney. I do some of the other things. When you are in business law is all around you. Whether you are handling this particular lawsuit or handling other business a knowledge of the law is key.

HB: Did you learn to fly in the R22?

KR: Yes. I learned to fly when I got out of college.

HB: Do you own your own, or when you want to fly, do you just use a company ship?

KR: We put a minimum of 5 hours on all of our ships at the factory. Generally our flight test is done after about 3 hours, so they need another 2 hours flying. They are always leaving me messages about ships they need to fly, so I will take one of those.

We take a ship every summer up to my father's place in Seattle. It tends to have some new - whatever it is we are trying out - on it. That becomes the factory demonstrator. I don't own one and probably never will because they are at the factory.

HB: Some R22s seem somehow to fly more smoothly than do others. Is there an explanation for that?

KR: There are two components that will make a variation in the aircraft. One is the engine and one is the blades.

Blades and the way they are matched is an art. Some of them have a better match and tend to be smoother and maybe fly a little faster. The same with engines. Lycoming deliver engines which have a range that they can operate in. So if you couple a really good engine with a really good matching set of blades you can get a ship that turns out to be a little faster, a little smoother than others. That's really what it is.

We take great pains as a company to make certain that all aircraft meet a minimum quality level. Within that there may be some variation. Certainly after an aircraft has been out in service for a year or two the way that it is maintained, the way they do the track and balance, that can really affect a ship over the life of it. I've seen ships that are really well maintained flying at 2100 hours and they fly like a brand new ship, really smooth and nice. And I've seen other ships where it's pretty obvious they weren't tracked and balanced and after a couple hundred hours they feel like they need an overhaul.

We have always said if you have a good mechanic you'll never have problems with the ship and it will be a great ship. If you don't have a good mechanic then you are going to have problems.

Ever affable, **Kurt Robinson** takes time out on a busy Friday afternoon to stand in front of the RHC headquarters for a photo.

HB: Have you got a favourite R22 from your past?
KR: The favourite ship that you have is the ship that you are flying at the time. I've done quite a bit of cross-country flying. I've taken ships to Florida. I took an R22 up to Edmonton, Canada with a couple other guys. It was just a wonderful trip. There was another R22 and a 44 and we flew as a flight of three. Through

Las Vegas, up through Utah and all the way up to Canada. By the end of the first day you've got your ship and you just love it. By the time I had to deliver it I felt like it was my ship and didn't want to give it up.

HB: You have said that you believe the R44 is easier to fly than the R22.
KR: It is because you have a higher inertia rotor system. In a sense it slows down the manoeuvres and the time required to respond to things. Although the aircraft is faster than the R22, doing landings and autos you have more time to accomplish things in the R44. You don't have to be as quick on the reactions as on the R22.

The R22 is quick; it's a sports car. It's a less forgiving aircraft. Everything you do you have to be right on top of: there is less margin for error. Once you learn on the R22 you carry that knowledge over to other ships.

HB: When I've asked other pilots about possible improvements to the R22 they tend to scratch their heads. But, what about fitting a glass [electronic] cockpit?
KR: We are not looking at that now, but that is probably the area as time goes on that we will look at. Certainly as new GPS come on and new things like that we will look to incorporate those into the helicopter. The same thing with the glass cockpit. If they turn out to be lighter, easier to read, if they truly reduce the pilot's workload, we could add those on. What we won't do is just throw on gimmicks because it's the latest thing. In fact Frank is dead set against that. We are very structured in what we look at. If you look at the avionics in the R22 and R44 it is all pretty state of the art.
The reason I pointed out weight is that it is something that would make any engineer in the company show interest. If you came to me and said that you've got a new alternator that will put out the

same voltage but is five pounds lighter, we'll go okay, we'll take a look at it. But it can't be *just* that. You've got weight, cost and reliability. So you are constantly looking at all three of those items and saying you require all three.

I've already had vendors come up to me at the show [Helitech] touting one of the three, and they want you to try their product. Then you ask them about the other two and when they won't talk about the other two you say oh well, I need all three. Certainly whenever we find all three then that is a good candidate for an update on any of our helicopters.

HB: Finally, I have seen vendors selling their own parts for the R22, full bubble doors and external oil coolers and so on. Do they require your approval?
KR: There are certain items that have received FAA approval for our helicopters. It's called an STC [Supplemental Type Certificate]. We really have no involvement in it. We don't because we don't want to pick up the liability. If we decide to do something we tend to do it totally in-house because we are going to be responsible for it.

HB: Thanks very much for your time.
KR: You're welcome.

These ground wheels are altogether larger than the originals. It requires more force to flip over the lever, but produces greater lift. With the larger diameter wheels the R22 is higher off the ground and easier to push. However, they will not fit under the seat to carry along as do the RHC originals which is very handy when landing away.

Left, is a non-RHC full length bubble door. It creates more shoulder and hip room. The window within the framework opens by sliding down. The drawback is that the framework actually reduces visibility through the upper half compared with the original door with fixed window.

Also, bubble doors like pop-out floats can decrease cruise speed by 5 knots.

The standard R22, like s/n 3453 above, without bubble windows or floats, is the most aerodynamically efficient. The shape of the 22 is one of its great assets: form and function working in harmony.

This remote oil filter carries an FAA Supplemental Type Certificate. It was fitted to a 0-320 engine in a Beta which originally did not come with an oil filter. The cartridge is held vertically so there are no drips when it is renewed. This model also has a metal chip warning light system to warn of metal particles within the engine. It worked perfectly for years, but when it arrived in the UK it had to be removed. For some reason FAA STCs are not accepted by the CAA.

Where to Fly

I'm leaving because the weather is too good.
I hate London when it's not raining.

                                    Groucho Marx

It can be frustrating; not the too good weather that Groucho is re-
ferring to, but the rain. Not to mention the fog, mist and low
cloud. Sometimes you want to blast a hole in the sky to let the
clear blue through at last.

It might seem surprising that there are any flying enthusiasts in the
UK at all. Yet there are many. Don't forget that this is the home
of the Spitfire, Concorde, and the Lynx helicopter world speed
record holder. Every summer thousands of ordinary people turn
out for air shows to see these and other aircraft. So, if you live in
the UK, where could you fly your R22, weather permitting of
course?

You can fly over cathedrals and castles, great houses and gardens,
Hadrian's Wall, Devil's Dyke, stone curlews, Stonehenge, iron
age forts, windmills, watermills and the white cliffs of Dover.
And oddly enough, you can fly the river Thames through the heart
of London. It is true that you will be busy with various Air Traffic
Controls in the process, but then most airspace above the UK
seems to be under someone's control. The positive side of this is
that almost every small airfield has Air Traffic Control waiting to
help you, or let you know when you've gone wrong.

Many Europeans train in the United States, and especially Florida.
Its year-round good flying weather means that you fly every day,
seven days a week, except for the odd hurricane of course, and

In this photo the R22 is heading down river with London Bridge in the foreground and Tower Bridge straight ahead. Continuing east a further 6 miles is London City Airport which is, unfortunately, not available for use by helicopters. The heli-route ends at the Isle of Dogs, before reaching the airport. The warship is H.M.S. Belfast.

even then, between hurricanes the weather is good. There are plenty of helicopter flying schools, and the facilities are very good. Even airfields without an Air Traffic Service Unit of any kind have concrete runways on which to practice running landings.

And from the air there is mile after mile of white sandy beach and aqua-blue ocean. Inland there are waterways, canals, orange groves and alligators. The alligators are no problem from the air, but watch out for six foot wide turkey buzzards that, like humans, go south for the winter. They are at the top of the food chain and have no fear. That applies to the turkey buzzards as well.

Heading up the Thames, Westminster Bridge and the Houses of Parliament are in the Centre, with Lambeth and Vauxhall Bridges respectively in the distance. London Battersea Heliport is another three bridges beyond. Strict heli-routes apply in central London. Only police and emergency medical helicopters are permitted to fly freely inside The Specified Area... and the Queen of course.

In the summer, however, the Florida noon-day sun would only tempt mad dogs and Englishmen. Even doors-off flying at 1000 feet is hot, and with high humidity you still need to monitor carb heat. If you prefer a temperate climate and a variety of terrain, then Southern Florida may not be for you.

When you return to the cool air and undulating hills of England you may find that some flying schools can be a bit sniffy about your having trained in the US. If so, take your custom elsewhere. After all, there are only so many manoeuvres you can do in a helicopter, so what does it matter where you do them?

If you live in Southern California you have the advantage of good weather, blue ocean with sandy beaches, flat deserts, hills and mountains. You will also have plenty of company. There are more helicopters in California than in most countries. Safe to say that the location of the Robinson factory has impacted on this statistic. Maintaining your R22 will be considerably easier close to the source of parts, and when it reaches 2200 hours, how much more convenient and economical to fly it to the factory for rebuilding rather than crating and shipping it. You can probably operate an R22 in Los Angeles for half of what it costs in the UK.

Looking east towards the Atlantic, the waterway in the foreground is Florida's Intracoastal Waterway which runs for miles along the southern Florida coast. From an R22, doors off, you can see sharks basking in the warm water.

Boca Raton Inlet, above, is within Boca Raton controlled air space. If you fly south along the beach you are kept busy talking, one right after the other, to Air Traffic Control from Palm Beach International, Boca Raton, Pompano Beach, Fort Lauderdale, and Miami. By the time one of them has given permission to enter their airspace you are already asking permission to leave and change frequencies to the next. Since aircraft coming the other way are doing the same thing, there may be no overlap which would give you advance warning of traffic coming your way. Even at a modest speed of 75 knots each, the two aircraft are closing at a velocity of 150 knots. One moment you scan and there is nothing there. The next moment suddenly there is.

Your Good Health

I eat the air, promise-crammed.
Hamlet III.ii.98

A great many things change when you lift away from the earth. The temperature decreases, humidity decreases, pollen decreases, but negative ions increase. Any or all of these can be better for your health.

Unless there is an inversion, the **temperature** will drop as you ascend, usually at the accepted lapse rate of 2° C for every 1,000 feet. This is because the atmosphere itself takes on virtually no heat from the sun's rays. The atmosphere is warmed from below by the ground. The ground absorbs solar heat and transfers it up into the atmosphere. So the temperature is warmest near the heat source, the ground, and decreases as you move further away.

Most people will find this decrease in temperature mildly stimulating, a bit like lowering the car window. On a hot day it can make you feel significantly more comfortable. On a very hot day you may feel and perform better because heat can have a deleterious affect on the body. The body tries to cool itself by bringing blood to the surface to release heat. This means that there is relatively less blood available for muscles, internal organs and the brain. Fatigue may set in with a loss of mental capacity. Judgement and performance can suffer.

The effect of heat is greatly exaggerated if there is high **humidity.** Heavy, humid air can make you feel drowsy and lethargic. The body also controls its temperature by sweating. If the water vapour in the atmosphere is very high, evaporation of sweat from the skin is inhibited and is less effective at lowering body temperature.

The water vapour capacity of air is determined by temperature. Warm air with 80% humidity contains more water vapour than cold air of 80% humidity. So as the helicopter ascends the temperature decreases and so does the humidity. You feel better because dryer air is more comfortable than humid air.

Humid air is also less dense than dry air. A fixed volume of gas at a constant temperature and pressure will always contain the same number of molecules whatever the gas. So if water vapour (which don't forget is a gas) is added to dry air, some other molecules will be displaced. Air is made up of approximately 78% nitrogen, 21% oxygen and 1% mixed gases. Water vapour molecules have a lighter atomic weight than both nitrogen and oxygen molecules. So humid air is actually lighter than dry air, and it contains less nitrogen and oxygen, as some of those gas molecules have been displaced by the water vapour molecules. Our bodies prefer to breathe oxygen rather than water vapour, so you will feel better in lower relative humidity. The recommended range for comfort is 30% to 60%.

What we breathe in affects how we feel and perform. At ground level you breathe in more undesirable **pollen** and pollutants. Plant pollen, seeds and even small insects can be swept up by the wind and carried to amazing heights, but that is the exception. As a rule most pollen stays near the ground so that deposition of pollen in and around the source plot is much greater than outside it.

If you are one of the many sufferers of hay fever, asthma, or similar respiratory complaints you may feel better in yourself when you are transported up and away from substances that trigger these allergies. Gravity acts to pull the pollen down to earth.

Cooler temperatures in the evening also help pollen to settle out. But, the best way to remove pollen from the air is with a rain shower.

A rain shower brings other health benefits as well in the form of **negative ions**. Ions are charged particles that occur naturally in the air. They are formed when a neutral atom gains or loses an electron. They are generated by cosmic rays, ultraviolet radiation, water in motion, waterfalls, rain storms, windstorms and the like. The ions may be either negatively charged or positively charged. Positively charged ions, curiously, have a negative affect on humans.

Positive ions are found in increased numbers in, for example, cities, next to congested motorways, near cathode ray tube computer monitors, and in wind storms. Hot, dry wind storms such as the Chinook in the Rocky Mountains fill the air with positive ions. (The Chinook helicopter is named after the Chinook tribe of Native North Americans, not from the wind). During these storms many people develop headaches, nausea, anxiety, irritability and respiratory trouble.

That wind storms have this affect was known before scientists suggested that it was due to positive ions. Raymond Chandler, in one of his short stories, *Red Wind,* published in the 1930s, describes the affect with his usual sharpness:

> "There was a desert wind blowing that night. It was one
> of those hot dry Santa Anas that come down through
> the mountain passes and curl your hair and make your
> nerves jump and your skin itch. On nights like that every
> booze party ends in a fight. Meek little wives feel the
> edge of the carving knife and study their husbands' necks.
> Anything can happen."

If you live in such an area, during weather like this, best leave your R22 in the hangar.

Not all charged ions are detrimental to health. Negatively charged ions have the opposite affect. Negative ions freshen and clean the air. They neutralise odours, and cause airborne pollen and viruses to become heavy enough to settle out of the air. They decrease anxiety and improve energy and mental clarity. They help alleviate depression and lift mood.

Why negative ions do this is not completely understood. Apparently, among other things, negative ions in the blood stream improve and accelerate the oxygen uptake at cellular level. More oxygen at cell level means improved health and well being. Highly charged environments of negative ions also stimulate the nervous system, although exactly how is not yet fully explained.
Where do these beneficial negative ions naturally occur? Many of them occur where helicopter pilots often fly: in the country, over pine forests, along the seashore, in the mountains and near waterfalls. Admittedly waterfalls are outside the range of most pilots. But, for those lucky enough to fly near them, the concentration of negative ions goes from 2,000 per cubic centimetre in ordinary air, to 100,000 per cc close to a large waterfall.

This may help to explain that mood lift and good feeling you experience after flying an R22. It is not just from the fun of flying it and the stunning panoramic views you get. Lifting off the ground and flying into cooler, less humid air away from pollen and pollution and into increased numbers of negative ions is good for your health. And it is a plausible story to tell people who ask why you need to go flying regularly. It's for health reasons. Really.

The improved state you are in when you return to earth in your R22 is somewhat similar to one of Einstein's theories about returning to earth after an extended flight. He theorized that someone travelling away from earth at the speed of light would return to earth younger than someone who did not take the flight and remained on earth. The traveller would have gone further in the space direction than in the time direction. Time in their reference frame would be shorter than that of the earthbound person, even though they would have both arrived at or returned to the same space-time point. So the person who left the earth would be younger than the person who stayed behind.

Similarly, when you return to earth after a flight in an R22 you will feel younger and fresher than if you'd remained on the ground, even if you didn't fly at a speed of 186,000 miles per second. You couldn't really enjoy the view at that speed anyway.

Above: Small rural aerodromes can literally bring a breath of fresh air into your life. Open green space, surrounding trees and fields, and no smog. This aerodrome cannot boast of a single paved runway, but that limits the number of fixed wing aircraft that are able to use it, which is good for helicopters.

It may appear in this photo that the pilot is coming in wide of the 26L runway, but he is heading for the 26 heli-strip situated to the left of the runway. There are helicopter strips adjacent to east-west and north-south runways, as well as four separate helicopter training areas and a hover square. Redhill is helicopter friendly.

The air is better up here. This green and pleasant landscape is to the south of London. In the far distance is the white concrete of Gatwick Airport in West Sussex.

Gatwick class D airspace seems to take up a considerable area of southeast England. Most general aviation pilots choose to fly around it. However, if Gatwick Air Traffic Control have time, and if you are patient and deft at changing radio frequencies, they will allow your R22 to take a short-cut over their active runway, in be-tween landing 737s. (Yikes!)

Greatness

The test of the machine is the satisfaction it gives you. There isn't any other test. If the machine produces tranquillity it's right. If it disturbs you it's wrong until either the machine or your mind is changed.

Robert M Pirsig
Zen and the Art of Motorcycle Maintenance

Channel 5 in the UK televised a program called "The World's Greatest Helicopters." Contributors included an aircraft historian, a journalist, a helicopter designer, a test pilot, a pilot record holder, and a novelist. These were their top ten selections in descending order:

10th	**Erickson Air Crane**
9th	**Lama**
8th	**Chinook**
7th	**Jet Ranger**
6th	**Sea King**
5th	**Westland Lynx**
4th	**Mil 26**
3rd	**Apache Longbow**
2nd	**Robinson R22**
1st	**Bell UH-1H "Huey"**

Some of the reasons given for making the Huey number one were that it is everyone's vision of a helicopter, you can do anything with it, 5500 were made by Bell, plus thousands more made under production rights, it has longevity and legendary toughness, and there is no mistaking the whop-whop-whop of its rotor blades.

It is hard to disagree with most of those claims. It is certainly true that the R22 is never going to match the sound of the Huey - unless you fixed loud-speakers to it and played a recording of the Huey at full volume. Nor has production of the R22 reached 5500 units, but it has already passed the 4000 mark, notwithstanding that it is a civilian helicopter. As to the claim that you can do anything with a Huey, how about pushing it in and out of the hangar by yourself? There is no disputing, however, that it is an absolute classic.

Of course there is the question of which dictionary meaning of the word "great" is being applied? "Distinguished" and "famous" certainly fit the Huey, but "much in use or favour" is a perfect match for the R22. These "world's greatest" competitions are just for fun anyway. They stimulate discussion, but by their very nature will always be a matter of opinion. So let's look now at some opinions of the Robinson R22.

The person who really outshone all the others on the program when assessing the R22 was Quentin Smith, who spoke with real feeling. He avowed that the introduction of the R22 produced a "revolution" in the helicopter market. That it made travelling by helicopter "seriously practical as personal transport." The R22 can do this because: "It's affordable, it's reliable, it's efficient, it's fast, it's practical." In short it is, "just brilliant."

It was never made clear whether the other contributors were pilots or not. A great helicopter on paper, and a great helicopter to fly may not be the same thing. Clearly personal experience makes for a more informed and meaningful opinion. The two judges who were known to be helicopter pilots were the most enthusiastic about the R22. Chances are that like thousands of others around the world, unless they learned to fly in the military, they probably learned on the R22. Even when pilots go on to a larger and more powerful helicopter, they still tend to view the R22 with great affection. Randy Rowles, typically, began his flying career in an R22 Alpha.

Based on the success of the Bell 47 as a medical evacuation helicopter during the Korean War, the U.S. Government invited companies to design a helicopter to meet new higher specifications. Bell had their prototype in the air by the late 1950s and won a contract for 200 of them. It was designated a Helicopter, Utility, model 1A, or HU-1A. The army named it the Iroquois, but to this day everyone calls it the **Huey**.

As the US became more involved in the conflict in Vietnam, Hueys became not just medevacs, but gunships and troop transporters. Millions of people around the world watched them in action on television news reports.   As a result the Huey became arguably the most recognizable helicopter in history. The same could be said for the sound of its 48 foot diameter rotor blades.

Thirty years later it may not have the resonance it once did, especially for young people. As a restored private aircraft it is rather an expensive proposition, but the Huey above, which is in private hands, is a very popular guest at air shows.

No helicopter has yet surpassed the 249 mph (400 kmph) world speed record set by this Westland Lynx, G-LYNX, in 1986. The experimental rotor blades were designed specifically to cope with high speed and the vibration and stresses that it produces. The Lynx is powered by two Rolls-Royce Gem turboshaft engines. Even the ordinary off-the-shelf Lynx is good for 200 mph.

The Chinook has to be one of the most entertaining helicopters to watch. Standing still the limp rotor blades droop like over-long diving boards on collision course. Yet, somehow the fore and aft blades never strike. And when they are in motion they appear to be at warm-up rpm when suddenly the aircraft lifts. You think you could almost run in circles and keep up with them. This RAF Chinook performed aerobatics at Biggin Hill Airshow.

Randy Rowles, on the right, has examined and passed a great many helicopter pilots, including myself, but perhaps none so memorable as the elated man above who, having trained on the R22, has just completed his certification on the Bell 206 Jet Ranger. It is the 6th December, 1997. The man is Harrison Ford.

The R22 was the first helicopter that I trained in. It was the Alpha model. The Robinson provided an opportunity to get my training. I couldn't afford anything else.

It also provided my first job. The first job I had upon completing my commercial was aerial application crop dusting. It was a tremendous learning environment. This was back before they had governors in the R22. It was all manual throttle. I learned a lot about power management. I also learned a lot about limitations.

Just because we used the Robinson for crop dusting doesn't mean that we should have used it. Every mission deserves the proper aircraft. I don't now feel that the R22 probably should have been doing the work that it was doing, at the volume that we were doing it. Now the R44 is much more suited.

I have the opportunity to fly many different aircraft. I still enjoy the R22. Doors off, wind blowing through your hair, it's a great feeling. It's very responsive. It is just an all round fun helicopter to fly. As long as it is flown within its limitations and within the limitations of the pilot it's a very safe helicopter. It has proven that time and again. I think the aircraft itself is perfect the way it is because to change anything would be to take it outside what it was designed for - a personal transportation helicopter.

Randy Rowles, Fort Worth, Texas

Another instructor, Kevin Rattey gives his opinion of the R22:

I learned to fly on the R22. I found it to be a sports car of helicopters because I had a little bit of Schweizer time, and the Robinson reacts much quicker. It's much quicker on the controls. The Schweizer tends to lag a little bit. Robinson gives you instant feed-

back. So I found that the ship itself demanded a lot of attention. It demanded that you stay on top of things and stay ahead of the ship.

I found the Robbie to be a good training ship because it demands that you respect the ship and learn to fly within its limits and you learn how to manage power. You get a lot of power when you pull collective. Things react very quickly so it is a good training platform to develop your skills and be on top of things.

Everybody will tell you that the Robinson is less forgiving than any other ship. If you make a mistake it doesn't give you as much leeway as a larger ship would. So I think it demands that you become a better pilot overall. It's not the most comfortable ship for long trips, but I can't really say anything against the Robbie because it's a very well built ship.

Kevin Rattey, Lantana, Florida

Two types of language emerge from these monologues. Emotive language such as "fun," "great feeling," and "brilliant," and de-notative language such as "reliable," "efficient," and "responsive." The first vocabulary is emotional and the second is scientific. Pilots can move back and forth between them and still know what they are talking about. Not everyone can do this. People tend to view the world either as a collection of feelings: the emotional view, or as a collection of facts: the scientific view.

Most people tend to be in one camp or the other. There are those that can balance an internal combustion engine until it purrs, but cannot balance the furniture arrangement in the living room. They can plumb in a bathroom, but will not think twice about where the units are placed nor how the pipe-work looks. They can see how things work, but not how they appear.

The flip side of this personality is the person who, like my mother, can see in an instant which necktie looks best, how to set the table for symmetry and counterpoint (although she would never use those words), and what carpeting pattern will best compliment the living room furniture and drapes.   At the same time when her car won't start, she is utterly unable to apply any logic or reasoning to determine why.

There are, however, people with a foot in each camp. People who have a curiosity about how things work. Who can apply themselves to understand how and why. Who possess an analytical brain, and can grasp meteorology, navigation, air law, flight performance and all the other subjects necessary to acquire a pilot's license. But if it were only the science of flight that interested pilots, they would be content to sit at a desk on the ground and read about it.

What makes pilots unique is that their scientific side is balanced by their romantic side. For what else is flying except pure romance, a passionate adventure, an exhilarating rhapsody in the blue. Not that you are ever likely to hear a pilot say such things. It doesn't fit with the desired insouciant plucky image.

French pilots are fortunate in this regard. When asked what it is like to fly a helicopter: *Qu'est-ce que vous pensez de voler un hélicoptère?* They can answer in a single word: *formidable.* It contains two levels of meaning: a formal definition which means, "considerable, fearful," and an informal, idiomatic sense which means, "terrific, fantastic." This may be only fitting since the English word, helicopter, is taken from the French, *hélicoptère.*

Of course an abundance of science is necessary to get that license to fly. But it is not the science that keeps pilots flying.   It is the romance of taking to the air. And if you are as fortunate as Frank Robinson and Chuck Yeager you may continue that romance into your seventies and eighties. As long as you look after yourself and pass your yearly medical, you will be fit and free to fly.

Think about it next time when it's a true blue sky of a day, and you've completed the pre-flight, set the altimeter, switched on the master switch and strobe, your hand poised on the ignition key. Ask yourself…

Where else would you rather be?

Selected Bibliography

Craig, Paul A, *The Killing Zone* (McGraw-Hill, New York, 2001). This is an analysis of General Aviation accidents concentrating on the high fatality zone of pilots' first 150 hours. Craig's purpose is to help pilots avoid these accidents. It is rather heavy on statistics, but they form the basis for his thesis that the most dangerous flying hours are the less experienced hours. Even though most examples are fixed wing, the sobering advice is relevant to all pilots.

LASORS - Licensing, Administration and Standardisation, Operating Requirements and Safety (Civil Aviation Authority, Gatwick Airport South, West Sussex, current edition). This is primarily a reference document regarding license requirements within the UK and Europe, now referred to as Joint Aviation Requirements(JAR). However, it also describes how to file a Flight Plan, and the Safety Sense section at the back is very broad, well written, down to earth and useful. It's hard to believe that it was produced by the CAA.

Padfield, Randall R. *Learning to Fly Helicopters* (TAB Books/ McGraw Hill, New York, 1992.)
I have avoided listing training books as every training school has their personal favourites. But this book is something more: accessible, interesting, personal, and written in an easy, non-didactic style. It will lift you up and get you back on track after a frustrating day.

Mason, Robert, *Chickenhawk* (Corgi Books, Great Britain, 1984)
If *Chickenhawk* were only about training to fly helicopters, or only about the Vietnam War, or only about a young man's journey through the highs and lows of war it would be very good. It's all of that and more.

Robinson R22 Maintenance Manual - And Instructions for Continued Airworthiness, (Robinson Helicopter Company, Torrance, California).
This is the manual used by maintenance organisations to maintain the R22. Not the ideal book to read in bed, mostly because if you prop it up on your chest you'll have trouble breathing: it weighs 2.4 kilos. But definitely worth having for reference, especially if you own an R22.
Contains some fault finding sections, and will enable you to communicate with engineers. Instead of talking about "that flat thingy at the end of the tailcone," you can refer to the "horizontal stabilizer." And if you really want to impress, work into the conversation that the horizontal stabilizer on your Beta has, of course, an increased angle of incidence, 2.8 to 3.3 degrees on its A023-20 tailcone as compared with the Standard, HP and Mariner's 1.8 to 2.3 degrees on the A023-1 tailcone. Mind, you may need to counterbalance that with an aside about how much weight you can bench-press so they don't think that you are just a part number nerd.

Robinson R22 Illustrated Parts Catalogue, (Robinson Helicopter Company, current as of date stamped on subscription form inside). Ever wondered how pushing the pedals translates into a tail rotor change? Turn to page 7-22 of the Parts Manual for an exploded drawing of how component parts interconnect. If your R22 is nearing a rebuild you may wish to read through the list of parts for the 2200 hour Field Overhaul Kit starting on page 12-11. Then check the price list at the back. Regular updates for both books are available by subscription from RHC. The Parts Manual and the Workshop Manual are sold as a pair.

Rotorcraft Flying Book, (FAA-H-8083-21, U.S.Department of Transportation, Federal Aviation Administration, 2000).
This A4 size colour illustrated book covers pretty much all helicopter exercises, and proves that government agencies can produce clear, concise and informative prose. And since it is deemed a public service book, there are no shareholders to demand a profit, so it is good value too.

Wolfe, Tom, *The Right Stuff* (Black Swan Books, London, 1989, Jonathan Cape, 1980) .
 As you no doubt already know, most of this book, subsequently made into a film, is about the astronaut training program. But, even if that is of only slight interest to you, bear in mind what prompted Wolfe to write this book, which was to determine why test pilots wished to fly, and to fly against such deadly odds. The second chapter is an excellent exposition on what it is like to want to fly.

Selected Internet Sites

It seems hardly worth listing helicopter sites because an internet search will probably lead to a zillion of them. Consequently these are just three noteworthy ones which also contain links to many others of interest.

www.griffin-helicopters.co.uk
This is a good all-round site which includes, among other things, a glossary of aviation abbreviations, FAQs for newcomers, self fly hire average prices in the UK, long, long lists of links, still photos, but probably of most interest are the video clips of air show displays, aerobatics, some minor accidents and some dreadful ones.

www.helicoptermuseum.co.uk
The museum containing "the world's biggest chopper collection" is in Weston-Super-Mare, England. It is informal, user friendly, and operates as a registered charity. Open Cockpit Days allow inside access to selected aircraft with an experienced guide. I am grateful to them for permission to photograph the R22 HP, the Hiller, and the World Record Lynx included in this book.

www.robinsonheli.com
If you fly a Robinson helicopter it is worth keeping a watching brief on the Robinson Helicopter Company site. The Customer Support section will keep you up to date on Safety Notices and Service Bulletins. There are recent press releases as well as the current price of a new R22. There is an interactive colour chart scheme for the R22, a chronological history of the company, a list of dealers around the world, and more.

About the Author:

H Brutlag trained for his Private Pilots License-Helicopter in both the UK and the US, and holds an FAA and a CAA license. He lives in London and flies his R22 out of Redhill Aerodrome in Surrey.

Previously he published *Vintage Sprint Bikes,* ISBN 0-9540361-0-7 about sprinting / drag racing vintage motorcycles.

Further information concerning that book can be found at: www.rennsport.freeserve.co.uk.

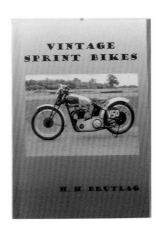

On the back cover:

This is a typical training school line-up of various colours and models of the Robinson R22 helicopter. Unusually, two of the four are IMC instrument trainer models, the red one in the foreground and the silver one behind it. The factory apparently did not keep records as to exactly how many of these were produced. Inevitably, some training schools will have two of them, and others none.